Spam and Scams Using Email Safely

Eric Minton

PowerKiDS press.

New York

Published in 2014 by The Rosen Publishing Group, Inc.
29 East 21st Street, New York, NY 10010

First Edition

Editor: Amelie von Zumbusch
Photo Research: Katie Stryker
Book Design: Colleen Bialecki
Book Layout: Joe Carney

Photo Credits: Cover Jose Luis Pelaez Inc/Blend Images/Getty Images; p. 5 Donald Iain Smith/Flickr/ Getty Images; p. 6 Jupiter Images/Comstock/Thinkstock; p. 7 Andresr/Shutterstock.com; p. 9 Mila Semenova/Shutterstock.com; p. 10 XiXinXing/Thinkstock; pp. 12, 17, 21 iStock/Thinkstock; p. 13 Prudkov/Shutterstock.com; p. 14 David Sacks/Lifesize/Thinkstock; p. 16 Ingram Publishing/Thinkstock; p. 18 VStock/Thinkstock; p. 19 Gawrav Sinha/E+/Getty Images; pp. 22, 26 Monkey Business Images/Shutterstock.com; p. 23 Dmitrijs Bindemanis/Shutterstock.com; p. 24 Hemera/Thinkstock; p. 25 AVAVA/Shutterstock.com; p. 27 Yellow Dog Productions/The Image Bank/Getty Images; p. 29 Goodluz/Shutterstock.com.

Library of Congress Cataloging-in-Publication Data

Minton, Eric.
  Spam and scams : using email safely / by Eric Minton. — First edition.
      pages cm. — (Stay safe online)
  Includes index.
  ISBN 978-1-4777-2934-2 (library) — ISBN 978-1-4777-3020-1 (pbk.) —
ISBN 978-1-4777-3091-1 (6-pack)
  1. Electronic mail messages—Juvenile literature. 2. Spam (Electronic mail—Juvenile literature. 3. Internet—Safety measures—Juvenile literature. 4. World Wide Web—Safety measures—Juvenile literature. I. Title.
  TK5105.73.M567 2014
  004.692—dc23
                              2013026331
Manufactured in the United States of America

CPSIA Compliance Information: Batch # W14PK2: For Further Information contact Rosen Publishing, New York, New York at 1-800-237-9932

Contents

"Email" is short for "electronic mail." Just as the post office lets you send postcards or packages to a person's street address, email lets you send information such as words, images, and videos to a person's email address.

Emails are sent much quicker than mail sent through the post office. They're also better than text messages for important conversations. Unlike texts, you can organize emails into **folders**. You can also use **search tools** to find specific emails.

However, you need to be smart when using email. If you're not careful, you could infect your computer with a **virus**. Someone might even trick you into giving him money or personal information. You need to know what to look for so that you don't get fooled.

How do you usually check your email? Some people tend to check their email on their phones, while others use tablets or computers.

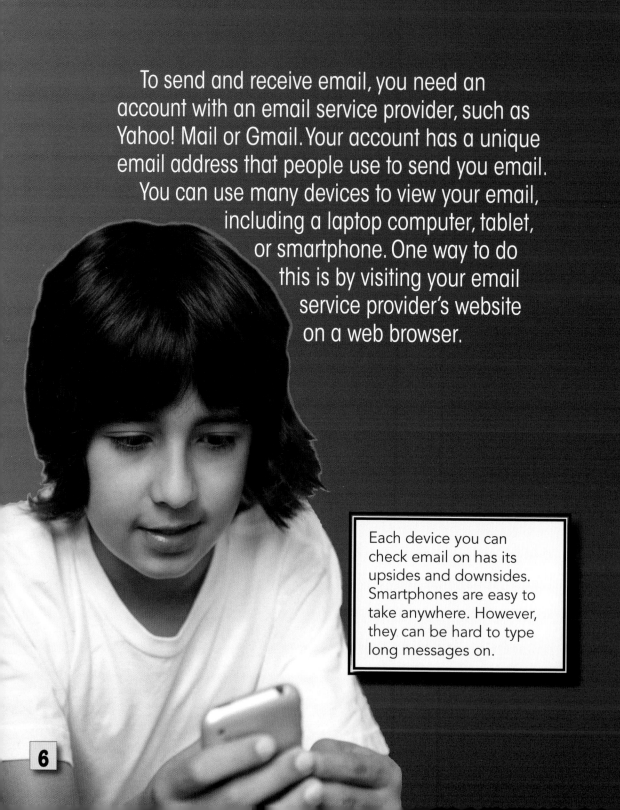

To send and receive email, you need an account with an email service provider, such as Yahoo! Mail or Gmail. Your account has a unique email address that people use to send you email. You can use many devices to view your email, including a laptop computer, tablet, or smartphone. One way to do this is by visiting your email service provider's website on a web browser.

Each device you can check email on has its upsides and downsides. Smartphones are easy to take anywhere. However, they can be hard to type long messages on.

Just as every person is unique, every email address is unique. After all, if two people had the same email address, their messages would keep getting confused.

Your email service provider may have an **app** that you can use to check your email on a tablet or smartphone. If you have more than one email account, computer programs such as Thunderbird, Microsoft Outlook, and Apple Mail put the emails from all of your accounts in one place.

Did You Know?

Each email address has two parts. The first is your user name. An @, or at sign, separates it from a domain name, like yahoo.com or gmail.com.

7

A **password** is a series of letters, numbers, and symbols you type to enter your account. Like the combination lock on a school locker, it is meant to keep unwanted people out. Anyone who knows your password can read all of your email, so never share it with anybody.

Make your password long and complex enough that no one can guess what it is. It should also be something that you can remember. If you have to carry it around on a slip of paper, someone else might read it and use it to get into your account.

If you have more than one email account, use different passwords for each one. That way, someone who learns the password to one account cannot get into all of them.

Email accounts are not the only things that use passwords. People also use passwords to log in to phones, tablets, and computers. Some websites require passwords, too.

When you create your account, you'll need to set up one or more security questions. These are questions that only you and those close to you would know the answers to. One example is, what is your mother's maiden name? If you forget a password, you can contact your provider to reset the password. When you do, you'll need to answer your security questions to prove that it's your account. This keeps other people from resetting your password to get into your account.

When answering a security question, you have to give the exact same answer you originally typed in. If you misspell the answer or can't quite remember it, you'll be stuck. Be sure you pick a question that you're sure you'll remember the answer to.

Security questions may ask facts about your family. What is your maternal grandfather's middle name? is one example. Your maternal grandfather is your mother's father.

A **hacker** is someone who breaks into email accounts or other computer systems. Hacking is a crime. While some hackers know a lot about computers, anyone you know can hack into your account if she can guess or steal your password. There are several signs your account may have been hacked. You may stop getting new emails. Your password may stop working.

If you get emails from a friend's account that do not seem like that friend really wrote them, her account may have been hacked. Contact your friend immediately.

12

Your email contact list includes the addresses of everyone to whom you regularly send emails. It can include friends, relatives, teachers, classmates, and more.

Emails that you didn't send could bounce back to your inbox. Friends may get emails from you that you didn't send. Your folders or **contact list** might change.

If you think that your account was hacked, change your password and your security questions immediately. Then run **antivirus software** in case the hacker put harmful software on your computer.

A link is an image or text that you click on to take you to a website. Text links look different from the surrounding text. For instance, they may be underlined or change color when you roll your cursor over them.

Email makes it easy to share group photos from family gatherings. Just send everyone in the group an email and attach the photo to it.

Send   Attach   Save as Draft

To: you@abc.com

From: me@xyz.com

Subject: This Book

Did you know this book has a website?
You can check it out at
www.powerkidslinks.com/sso/spam

Can you spot the link in this email?

An attachment is a computer file, such as a program or video, that has been sent as part of an email. You can click on an attachment to open or download it. Your computer can get a virus if you open a link to an infected website or open an infected attachment. Viruses can slow your computer down or allow a hacker to read or change anything that's on your **hard drive**. Links can take you to websites that automatically send viruses to your computer.

Email Spam

Spam is any kind of unwanted message that's sent to large numbers of people online. Some spam is advertising. Other spam is sent by **scammers** to trick you into giving them personal information. Spam often has file attachments or links that will give your computer a virus. Some viruses will make your computer send spam emails to all your contacts.

People who send you spam are most often trying to sell you something. This will frequently be something that you don't really want or need.

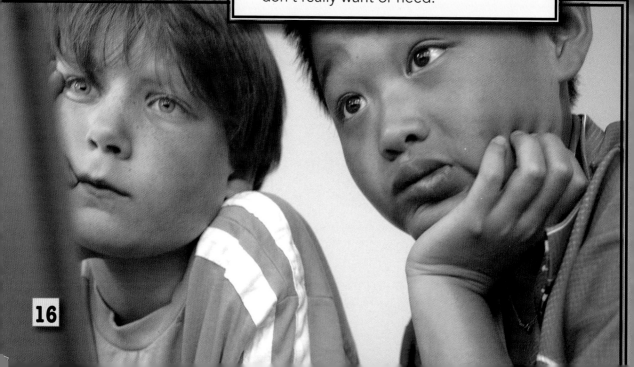

Emails that are full of bad grammar and misspellings or written in a foreign language are often spam.

It isn't always easy to spot spam. However, there are clues to look for. Emails from senders you don't recognize may be spam. Spam often contains links to websites. Beware of messages that ask you to buy something or send money. Messages asking for passwords or credit card numbers should set off your alarm bells.

Did You Know?

Almost 70 percent of emails sent in 2012 were spam, with spammers sending more than 30 billion spam emails every day.

17

Ask a parent or other trusted adult to help you set up your account's spam filter.

Sorting through your emails to weed out spam can take up a lot of time. Luckily, there are programs, called spam filters, that are designed to spot spam and put it into a special folder. This is called a spam folder.

Even if you use a spam filter, spam emails will sometimes slip past your filter and get into your inbox.

If you mark those messages as spam, it can help your spam filter learn to identify spam correctly.

Spam filters sometimes send genuine messages to your spam folder by accident. Check your spam folder regularly to see if important email is in there. If you find one, mark it as not spam. That should help the filter recognize messages from that sender in the future.

If an email you were expecting hasn't shown up in your inbox, check your spam folder. Your spam filter may have mistakenly directed the email there.

Other Sorts of Spam

Not all spam arrives by email. In **social media**, strangers may try and friend you so that you'll see the spam that they post on their profiles. Spammers send links on instant messaging programs, chat rooms, and online games. They also post links on forums, message boards, and blog comments. On video-sharing sites, spammers may post videos that are actually advertisements.

Social-media spammers try to lure you in by saying nice things about your posts or by describing a link as cool or funny. They may act like they know you even though they are strangers. They may even hack into a friend's account and post under your friend's name. Only click on links on social-media sites if you're sure that they are safe.

Spammers often leave comments that seem out of place. For example, a spammer might write about a moneymaking scheme in the comments for a music video.

Gone Phishing

When someone tries to trick you into giving him personal information, it is called **phishing**. If you get phished, you'll get an email or instant message that looks like it is from a real website, such as a social-media site or online game. The message tells you to click on a link to confirm or supply personal information, such as your real name, address, phone number, or password. The link takes you to a fake website.

If you are unsure if an email is from a real company, you can always ask a parent to call that company and ask if the company really needed to reach you.

If you think about it, phishing is a bit like fishing. The person phishing is like a fisherman, the phishing email is like bait, and the target is like the fish!

The hackers who set up these fake websites can use the information you give them to hack into your account.

If you get a suspicious email asking you for personal information, don't click on any links in it. Instead, go to the company's website directly by typing its address into your browser.

Did You Know?

Phishing also happens outside the Internet. Don't give personal information over the phone to a stranger who calls you, even if the call sounds like it's from a real company.

Once you send an email, you can't take it back. This is one reason why you should never write emails when you are angry. Any time you send an email, take a moment before you send it to reread it. This will help you make sure it says what you mean it to say.

Be careful not to hit Reply All unless you do really mean to. You don't want a personal reply to the sender to go to everyone who got that email.

Always check an email's address before you send it off. You don't want to accidentally send the email to the wrong person.

Don't say anything to someone by email that would be rude or hurtful if you said it face-to-face.

Always use proper spelling, grammar, capitalization, and punctuation in formal emails. **Emoticons**, such as :) and x_x, are okay to use in emails to friends but not in formal emails. Limit **acronyms**, such as LOL and IMO, to casual emails, too.

Did You Know?

When you are writing formal emails, always be clear and to the point. Remember to say what you're writing about in the subject line, too.

Some people strike out at former friends by sharing their personal emails with classmates. Having everyone know your secrets is embarrassing.

In person, your facial expression and tone of voice make the difference between jokes and insults clear. These don't come across in email, though. Avoid jokes that could come across as insults when writing emails.

Emails aren't always private. Anyone you send an email to can print it out or forward it to other people.

You can avoid a lot of problems in the long run if you always take a breath and think twice before sending an email.

Never write anything in an email that would embarrass you or hurt other people if it became public. Do not attach embarrassing or hurtful photos or videos to emails, either.

If someone hacks into your email account, she can read all your private messages. Delete any emails that would cause problems for you or other people if anyone else read them.

Did You Know?

Never send passwords or other personal information by email. Your email might get hacked. The person you're emailing might be careless with the information.

Email is a powerful tool. It offers a great way to keep in touch with friends and family. However, an email account is an important responsibility. If you're not careful, you can be publicly embarrassed, hackers can read your private files, or you can get a virus that damages your computer. Learning to avoid scams and viruses takes time, effort, and practice.

Your best defense against email scams is to be skeptical. Always think before you open an email or click a link. Don't assume that whatever you are reading is true. Spam, scams, and other email problems are less likely to catch you off guard if you are smart and well informed.

If an email makes you suspicious, do some research online. Sites like Hoax-Slayer and Snopes have information about common email rumors, viruses, and lies.

Be Smart and Safe

1. Typing in the wrong password too many times will temporarily lock your email account. This keeps hackers from guessing your password over and over until they get in.

2. Just as you need to lock a door to keep it secure, you need to log out of your email account whenever you finish using it.

3. A company will almost never ask you to click on a link to give them personal information. Emails that do are generally scams.

4. Links in emails from people you know aren't always safe. A friend may be fooled by a scam, or his account may be hacked to send spam.

5. Viruses can create pop-ups that link to fake antivirus websites. Only get antivirus software from reliable sources.

6. If you suspect an email from a friend is actually spam, talk to that friend. His account may have been hacked.

7. Never open a file attached to an email until you've run the file through an antivirus program.

Glossary

acronyms (A-kruh-nimz) Words made from the initials of several other words.

antivirus software (an-ty-VY-rus SOFT-wayr) A computer program that gets rid of harmful computer programs.

app (AP) A computer program made for mobile devices, such as smartphones and tablets.

contact list (KON-takt LIST) A group of email addresses or screen names.

emoticons (ih-MOH-tih-konz) Pictures drawn with keyboard characters to show feelings.

folders (FOHL-derz) Places where groups of related computer files are stored.

hacker (HA-ker) A person who breaks into email accounts or other computer systems.

hard drive (HAHRD DRYV) A computer part that stores information.

password (PAS-wurd) Letters or numbers used to get access to an account.

phishing (FIH-shing) Posing as a real company to trick people into sharing personal information.

scammers (SKAM-erz) People who try to trick people into doing things.

search tools (SERCH TOOLZ) Ways to search through something.

social media (SOH-shul MEE-dee-uh) Online communities through which people share information, messages, photos, videos, and thoughts.

virus (VY-rus) A program that harms a computer.

Index

A
account(s), 6–8, 11–13, 20, 23, 27–28, 30
address, 4, 6, 22–23
antivirus software, 13, 30

B
browser, 6, 23

C
computer(s), 4, 6, 12–13, 15–16, 28

F
folders, 4, 13, 18–19

I
image(s), 4, 14
information, 4, 16, 22–23, 30

M
message(s), 4, 16–17, 19, 22, 27
money, 4, 17

P
password(s), 8, 11–13, 17, 22, 30
program(s), 7, 15, 18, 20, 30
provider, 6–7, 11

S
scammers, 16
search tools, 4
smartphone, 6–7
social media, 20

T
text(s), 4, 14

V
video(s), 4, 15, 20, 27
virus(es), 4, 15–16, 28, 30

W
website(s), 6, 14–15, 17, 22–23, 30

Websites

Due to the changing nature of Internet links, PowerKids Press has developed an online list of websites related to the subject of this book. This site is updated regularly. Please use this link to access the list: www.powerkidslinks.com/sso/spam/